Beginner Biography

Cesar Chavez
Friend to Farm Workers

by Jeri Cipriano
illustrated by Nigel Dobbyn

Look! BOOKS™

Red Chair Press   Egremont, Massachusetts

Look! Books are produced and published by Red Chair Press:
Red Chair Press LLC   PO Box 333   South Egremont, MA 01258-0333
www.redchairpress.com

FREE lesson guide at www.redchairpress.com/free-activities

Publisher's Cataloging-In-Publication Data
Names: Cipriano, Jeri S., author. | Dobbyn, Nigel, illustrator.
Title: Cesar Chavez : friend to farm workers / by Jeri Cipriano ; illustrated by Nigel Dobbyn.

Description: Egremont, Massachusetts : Red Chair Press, [2020] | Series: Look! books. Beginner biography | Includes index, glossary, and resources for further reading. | Interest age level: 006-009. | Summary: "As a child, Cesar Chavez worked on farms with his family. He felt the workers were not treated well. Cesar used his voice to become a leader in making sure farm workers were paid better and treated fairly"--Provided by publisher.

Identifiers: ISBN 9781634409698 (library hardcover) | ISBN 9781634409704 (paperback) | ISBN 9781634409711 (ebook)

Subjects: LCSH: Chavez, Cesar, 1927-1993--Juvenile literature. | Labor leaders--United States--Biography--Juvenile literature. | Mexican Americans--Biography--Juvenile literature. | Agricultural laborers--Labor unions--United States--History--Juvenile literature. | CYAC: Chavez, Cesar, 1927-1993. | Labor leaders--United States--Biography. | Mexican Americans--Biography. | Agricultural laborers--Labor unions--United States--History.

Classification: LCC HD6509.C48 C56 2020 (print) | LCC HD6509.C48 (ebook) | DDC 331.88/13/092 B--dc23

Library of Congress Control Number : 2019940524

Copyright © 2021 Red Chair Press LLC
RED CHAIR PRESS, the RED CHAIR and associated logos are registered trademarks of Red Chair Press LLC.

All rights reserved. No part of this book may be reproduced, stored in an information or retrieval system, or transmitted in any form by any means, electronic, mechanical including photocopying, recording, or otherwise without the prior written permission from the Publisher. For permissions, contact info@redchairpress.com

Photo credits: p 22: Everett Collection/Alamy

Printed in the United States of America

0420 1P CGF20

Table of Contents

The Early Years 4

Hard Times 8

Leader of Farm Workers 14

Strike for Rights 18

We Honor Cesar Chavez 21

Big Dates in Chavez's Life 22

Words to Know 23

Learn More at the Library 23

Index 24

The Early Years

Cesar Chavez was born in Yuma, Arizona, on March 31, 1927. He grew up on a big family farm. Cesar's best friend was his younger brother Richard. They rode horses. They played in the lake. They helped their father in the garden.

Cesar's family had come to Arizona from Mexico many years before he was born.

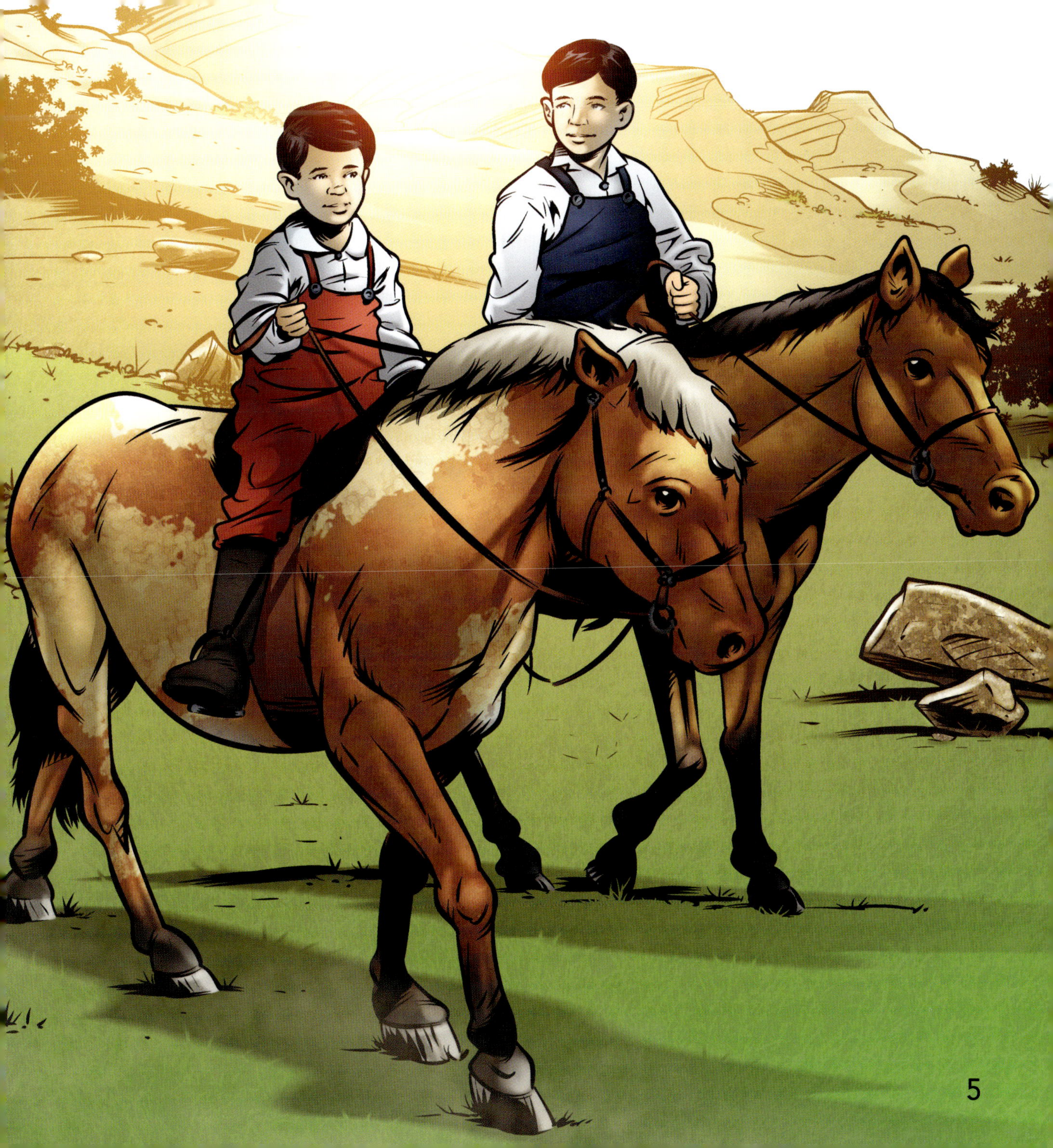

Cesar was not happy when he started first grade. Other children called him "dirty" because he had brown skin. Cesar's family was Mexican American. They had lived in the United States since the 1880s. Still, people were not kind to them.

Good to Know

In 1848, Mexico sold land to the U.S. That land makes up most of California, Texas, Nevada, Utah, Arizona, New Mexico, Colorado, and Wyoming.

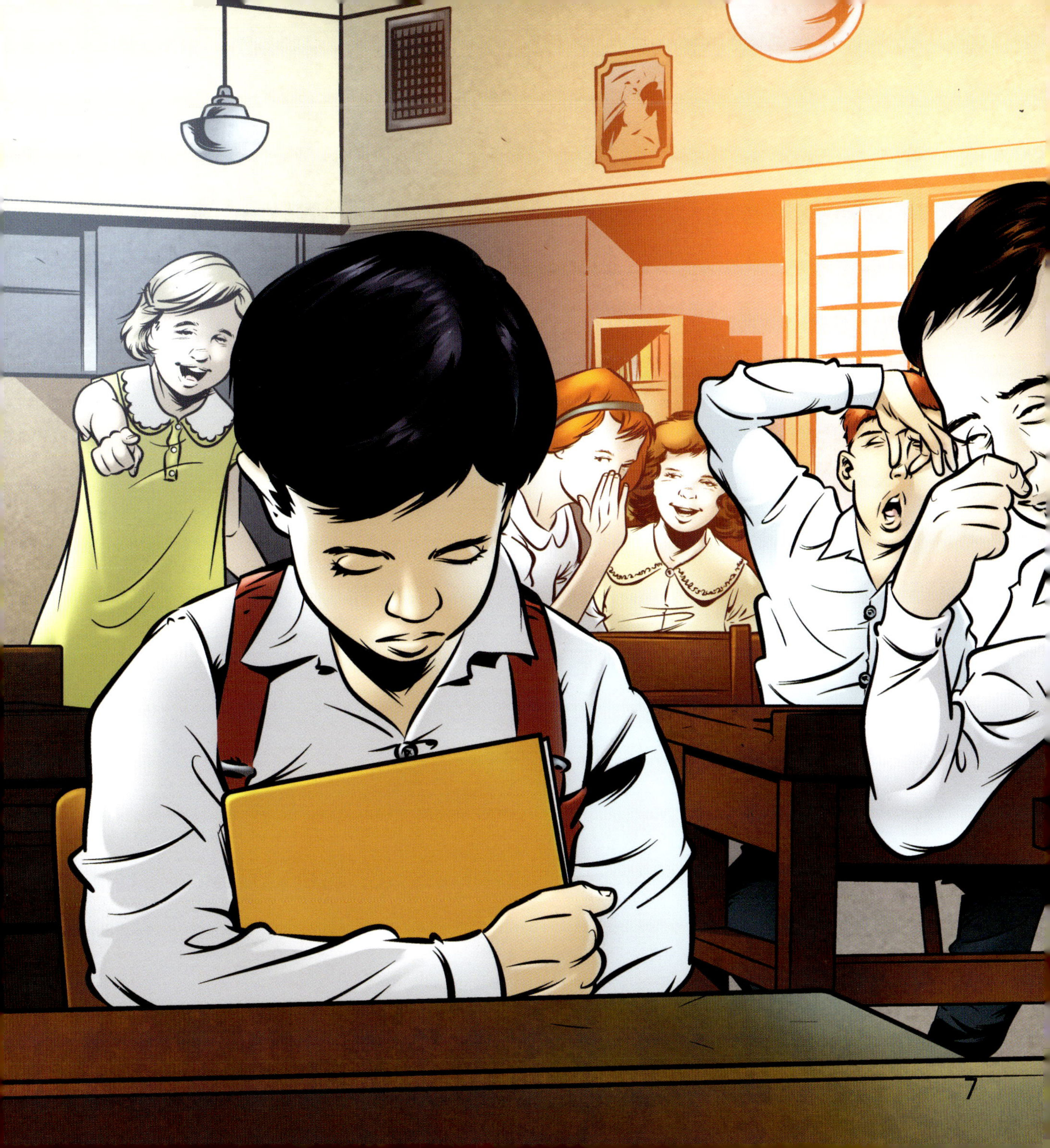

Hard Times

When Cesar was 10, the land got very dry. It did not rain. Crops died.

At first, the Chavez family was okay. They ate what they grew. But soon, they could not keep their farm. Like many other families, they drove to California to find work.

Many families drove to California to find work in the 1930s.

Cesar's family became **migrant** workers. They moved from farm to farm to pick crops. The family moved many times. Cesar went to 35 different schools. He left school after the eighth grade. He wanted to help his family in the fields.

Good to Know

The Chavez family—all eight of them—earned 30 cents a day. Today, that would come to less than $5.00.

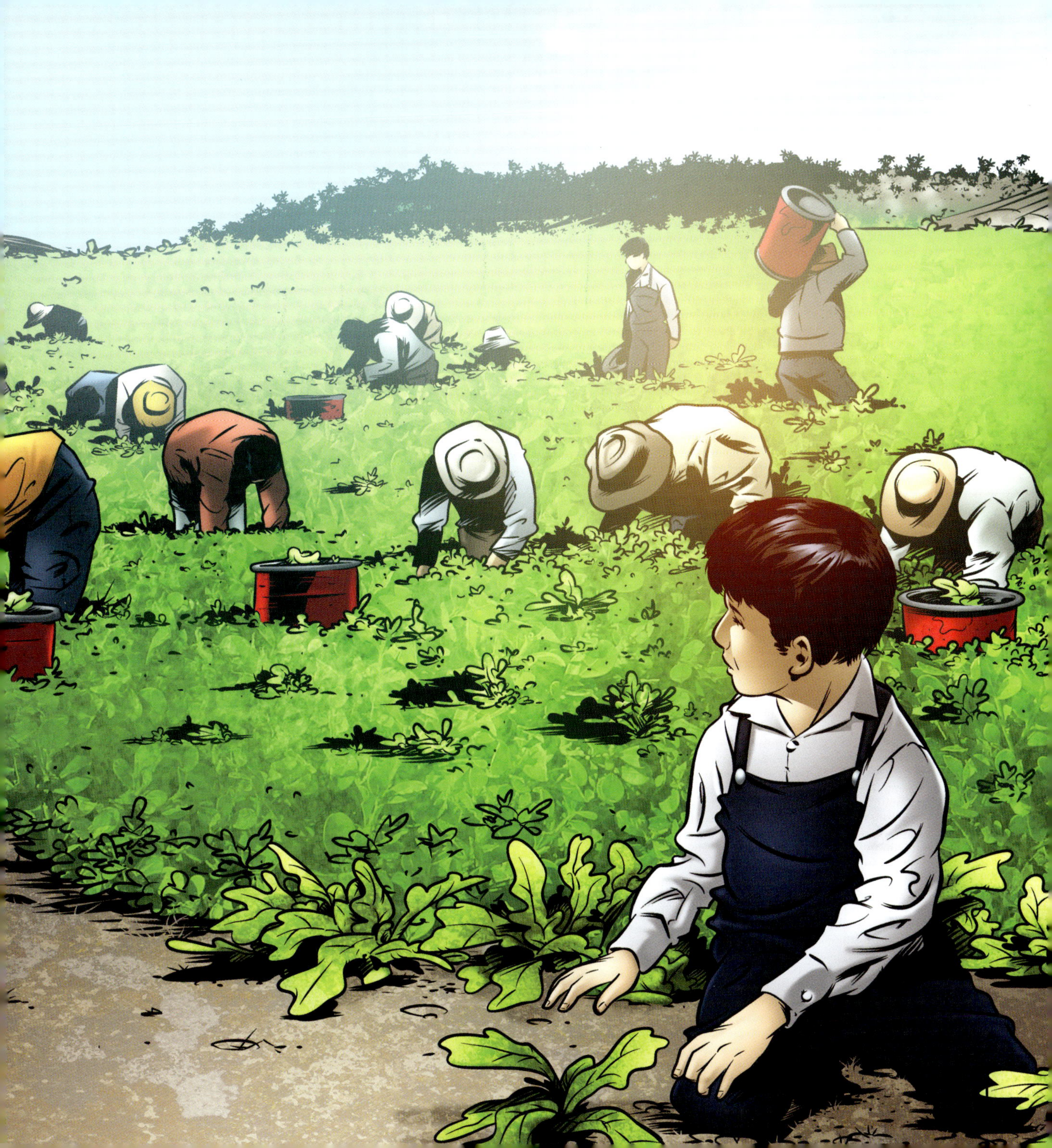

The Chavez family worked long hours. They lived in shacks with dirt floors. They shared a toilet and running water with others.

Life was hard. They worked in the hot sun. They had no water to drink. They breathed in bug-killing spray.

Cesar made up his mind. "Someday I will fix this!"

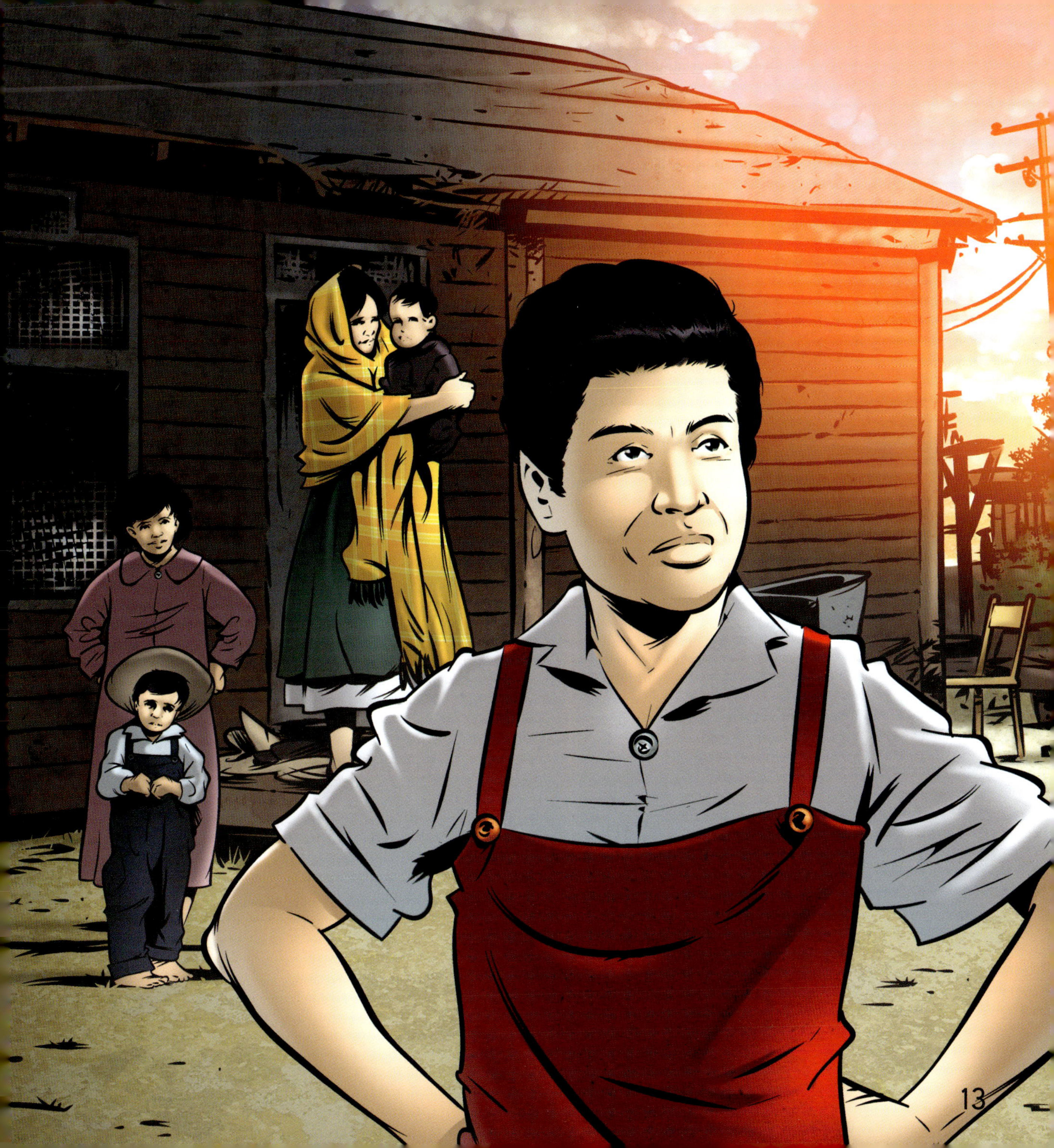

Leader of Farm Workers

When Cesar was 19, he joined the Navy. Then, in 1948, he married and started a family. Chavez helped people in the community. He went on to form the United Farm Workers of America (UFW) in 1962 with a woman named Dolores Huerta.

Good to Know

The new union needed a symbol. Cesar and his cousin made the picture. The eagle stands for courage. Red stands for **sacrifice**. White stands for hope.

In 1948, Cesar married Helen Fabela. Together, they started a family.

15

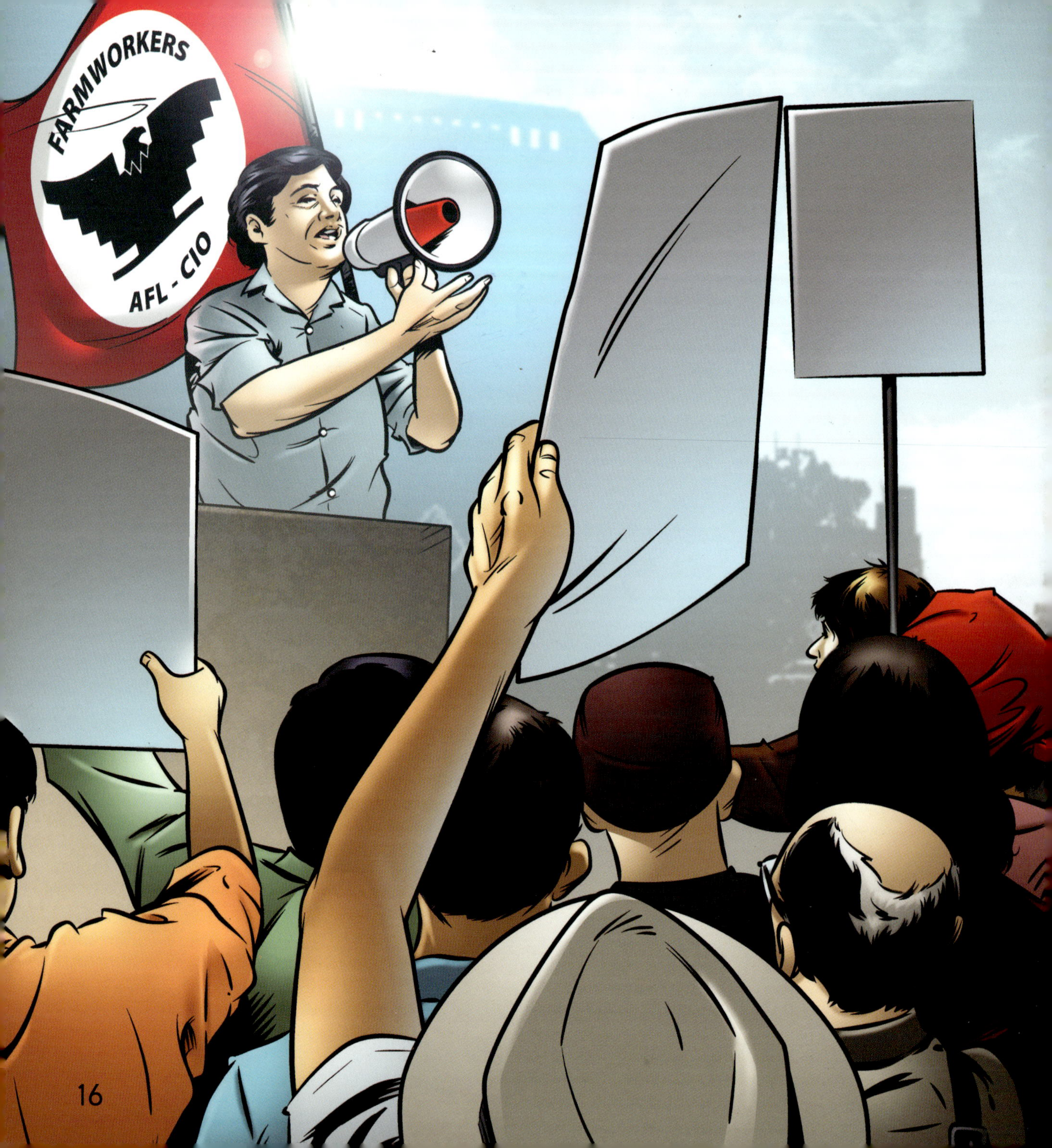
FARMWORKERS
AFL - CIO

Chavez gave farm workers hope. He led marches. The UFW motto was Sí se puede! "Yes, it can be done."

Chavez did not support fighting. When workers were bullied, he would stop eating. Once he **fasted** for 25 days to show that he believed in peaceful **protests**.

Strike for Rights

In 1965, grape pickers went on **strike**. Chavez led 67 men on a 340-mile march to the California state capital.

They walked 15 miles a day for weeks. Other farm workers joined as they walked by. When they reached the capital, there were 10,000 farm workers!

19

The strike lasted five years! People across the United States stopped eating grapes to show support.

Finally, in 1970, the growers gave in. They signed a **contract** with Chavez. Farm workers would get more money. They would have better working conditions too.

We Honor Cesar Chavez

Cesar Chavez died on April 23, 1993. More than 30,000 people came to his funeral.

In 1994, President Clinton honored Chavez with the Presidential Medal of Freedom. It is the highest honor a citizen can get.

In 2003, a postal stamp was made to honor Cesar Chavez.

Timeline: Big Dates in Chavez's Life

1927: Cesar Chavez is born in Yuma, Arizona.

1946: Chavez joins the U.S. Navy.

1948: He marries Helen Fabela.

1962: Chavez, his wife, and 8 children move to Delano, California.

1962: Chavez and activist Dolores Huerta form the National Farm Workers Association.

1965: Delano farm workers go on strike; the march to state capitol in Sacramento, California, grows to nearly 10,000 workers.

1970: Strike ends with higher pay and health care for workers.

1972: United Farm Workers Union is formed.

1993: Chavez dies, April 23 in San Luis, Arizona.

1999: He is elected to U.S. Labor Department Hall of Fame.

Words to Know

contract: a legal agreement

fasted: stopped eating food

migrant: a worker who moves from place to place to find work

protest: a show of being against something

strike: when workers refuse to work until something changes

united: joined together for the same purpose

Learn More at the Library

(Check out these books to read with others)

Krull, Kathleen. *Harvesting Hope: The Story of Cesar Chavez*, HMH Books for Young Readers, 2003.

Rau, Dana Meachen. *Who Was Cesar Chavez?* Grosset & Dunlap, 2017.

Roome, Anne and **Mattern, Joanne**. *Cesar Chavez: Champion for Civil Rights,* (Rookie Biographies) Scholastic, 2016.

Index

California................8, 18, 22
Huerta, Dolores................14
Medal of Freedom............. 21
Mexican American............. 6
Navy..........................14
United Farm Workers (UFW) ..14, 17
Yuma, Arizona 4

About the Author

Jeri Cipriano has written more than a hundred books for young readers. She enjoys reading and finding out new things. She likes to share what she learns.